DATING
OLD ARMY
PHOTOGRAPHS

ROBERT POLS

THE FAMILY HISTORY PARTNERSHIP

Published by
The Family History Partnership
PO Box 502
Bury, Lancashire BL8 9EP

Webpage: www.familyhistorypartnership.co.uk
Email: sales@thefamilyhistorypartnership.com

ISBN: 978 1 906280 27 7

First published 2011

Printed and bound by Information Press,
Southfield Road, Eynsham
Oxford OX29 4JB

Contents

Carte de visite; H Cooper, Leicester. Hussar's busby, shell jacket and lace braid are all in evidence on this portrait from the 1890s. (Carol Craggs collection)

Introduction

The family historian's ideal military photograph shows an ancestor whose regimental badge is clearly visible and readily identified. For some of us, of course, the dream comes true, and knowledge of the regiment opens up rich possibilities of further information. For many, however, the waking reality is rather less obliging. We may inherit a picture of a hatless soldier with no regimental insignia in sight. Or we may have a picture showing a cap badge, which we suspect holds the answer to all our problems, but which is infuriatingly out-of-focus. Examine it with a magnifying glass, and it's a blob; scan it and zoom in on it, and it's a pixellated blob.

But even if a soldier's photo fails to settle the regimental question, it may still have information to give. It may offer clues that help towards dating and that shed other, incidental light on the soldier's career. Such clues are the business of this book, which might more precisely have been titled *Dating and Learning from Old Army Photographs Even When You Can't Identify a Cap Badge*. It's a task that is undertaken with some trepidation, for this is the work of a photographic enthusiast rather than a military expert, and that fact is bound to show.

The complexities of dating from uniform are manifold. One might expect uniform to be easier to discuss and date than everyday civilian clothes. It is, after all, a matter of complying with regulations rather than a matter of making personal choices based on taste, fashion and cost. Uniform is, surely, uniform. But there were variations in practice from regiment to regiment. Styles adopted for service overseas found their way back for use at home. Uniforms authorised from a particular date were not always immediately issued, and officially obsolete items of uniform were sometimes slow to be discarded. The army, like any other family, had to get the wear from its clothing.

Inevitably, therefore, much of what follows is generalisation, applicable to most regiments but possibly subject to exceptions. Individual regiments are seldom mentioned, because it's assumed that regimental identification is a luxury that (to use an allegedly military turn of phrase) in our case we have not got. There is, however, a strong tendency to dwell on the infantry and the various military corps at the expense of the cavalry. This is partly because cavalry uniform seems to lend itself less readily to generalisation, and partly because the infantry and the corps accounted for more men and so generated far more soldiers' photographs.

But in spite of all these reservations and caveats, military expertise is not needed to find some useful dating clues in old pictures of soldiers. It is in that belief that the following pages are offered. They are the product of magpie eclecticism and owe much to authors cited in the bibliography. But they do represent a first attempt to focus on dating military pictures for family historians.

Finally, before letting the hungry reader move on to the main course, I am anxious to record my gratitude to Carol Craggs and Robin Stevenson for permission to reproduce photographs from their collections, and to my wife, Pam, for her customary patience in reading, questioning and commenting on what I have written.

Photographing soldiers

Though earlier single pictures of soldiers may exist, the first surviving set of military photographs appears to be a series of faded calotype portraits made in about 1843 by Captain Henry Brewster. In 1846 the Gordon Highlanders, stationed at Edinburgh Castle, provided David Hill and Robert Adams with eye-catching and sometimes dramatic subject matter. But Dr John McCosh, a surgeon in the army of the East India Company, favoured a more systematic approach. He began by making calotypes of his fellow officers during the Second Sikh War of 1848-9. He then added documentary photography to his repertoire, making pictures of troops and their equipment in the field (though not in action). He also argued that a British officer should learn to take and process his own photographs, in order to record the nature of the empire that he served. The Company agreed that photography was a suitable pastime for gentlemen and, early in the 1850s, ensured that officer cadets received tuition in its complexities before being sent out to India.

McCosh's pictures from the Second Burma War of 1852-3 were probably the first to capture images of a campaign. But the first military enterprise to produce a substantial photographic record was the Crimean War of 1854-6. Some small photographic expeditions to the Crimea were undertaken as early as 1854. Then, in 1855, Roger Fenton arrived on the scene with two assistants, five cameras, 700 glass plates, a darkroom wagon and four horses. He made and published over 300 images. Action pictures were out of the question, because the necessary exposure time was too long, but the photos nevertheless amount to an extensive documentary record that includes individual portraits, groups of eccentrically clad soldiers in camp, and the mutely eloquent view of a cannonball-strewn Valley of Death.

War photography was, nevertheless, still rather sanitised and could not yet depict events as they happened. That kind of immediacy had to await the American Civil War (1861-6) and the shorter exposures that were by then possible. But while war photography developed as a genre, the depiction of individual soldiers became the province of the commercial studio.

The earliest military studio portraits – daguerreotypes from the 1840s and 1850s, and ambrotypes from the 1850s – are generally of officers. Cost put them beyond the reach of other ranks. But in the carte de visite era (from the 1860s on) prices dropped, and the ordinary soldier – like the ordinary civilian – ventured with increasing frequency into the studio. At first, of course, the officer class was still more commonly photographed, but the carte de visite proved quite a speedy leveller.

Some practitioners came to specialise in military portraits. Robert Hills and John Henry Saunders built a chain of studios catering especially for the public school boy who went on to attend university or serve in the army. Their Eton business, which opened in 1864, was followed by branches in London, Cambridge, Harrow, Rugby, Sandhurst, Aldershot and York Town. The award of a first Royal Warrant in 1867 and a second in 1893 served to enhance their attraction to the target clientele. In London the officer class gravitated towards such society photographers as Camille Silvy, Alexander Bassano and Elliott & Fry. Beyond the capital, in towns with a regular martial presence, there were also professionals who aimed at the military market. J Vanhear of Portsea, for instance, promoted himself in the 1860s as 'Army and Navy Photographer', and in the 1870s Isaac Schofield of Colchester ran a 'Garrison and Camp Studio' as well as his original business.

There was also a market, extending beyond the family circle, in photographs of distinguished soldiers. During the carte de visite craze people collected portraits of the great and good to add to the more familiar faces that filled their albums. So soldiers – like royals, politicians and churchmen – appeared on cartes and, in due course, on cabinet prints, postcards and cigarette cards, for the edification of the general public.

Inevitably, where the army went the camera followed, with studios springing up to meet the needs of military men. In India, the earliest (albeit short-lived) studio was established in 1844, and by the end of the 1850s a number of businesses were thriving in the larger cities. Samuel Bourne, operating under his own name alone and as part of both 'Bourne & Shepherd' and 'Howard, Bourne & Shepherd', became associated with a chain of studios that encompassed Bombay, Calcutta and Simla. In Southern Africa, the first studio appeared in Port Elizabeth in 1846. For a quarter of a century this market was dominated by a modest number of Europeans and Indians, but after 1871 (and the invention of the dry-plate process) studios proliferated.

But if the maintenance of an empire lay behind the creation of many military images, the First World War lay behind the creation of many more.

Leaving for the front, returning on leave and – for the lucky ones – coming home to stay were all occasions to be recorded on camera. Studios equipped themselves for the martial boom by adding scenes of army camps with fluttering flags to their stock of painted backcloths. But amateur photography, too, now had a role to play. The 20th century's innovations had brought photography within the practical and financial grasp of Everyman, and families were able to create their own visual memories of sons and brothers who enlisted for the war. Some soldiers, in contravention of regulations, took the new and conveniently small Kodak Vest Pocket Camera to war with them. Amateur snaps from this time, however, have survived less often in family collections than the professional products.

Then, in its turn, the Second World War caused a further boom in pictures of soldiers. There were still many studios at hand, ready to mark the comings and goings, but by this time cameras in the family were not just possible but commonplace, and a wealth of amateur photographs have been handed down. Again, there were recruits who took their cameras to war, and this allowed the emergence of a new category of picture – the soldier as tourist – where combatants paused to pose in front of, say, the Sphinx or the Colosseum (just as their children did 20 or 30 years later, when ordinary people started to travel overseas for their holidays).

The military context

The reader does not need an extensive military background. Nevertheless, it's worth paying a little attention to the army and to the changes it experienced. This will introduce (if introduction is needed) some terms that will be encountered in the pages that follow. It will also show how significant changes in uniform related to unfolding events in the years that followed the birth of photography.

The army

The role of the Victorian and subsequent armies was threefold: it was needed for home defence; it was required to man the garrisons of an empire; and it was called on to fight wars. Arising from this mixed role comes a warning for family historians. If a soldier's photo can be dated to the time of a particular action, that doesn't automatically mean he was involved in it. A soldier photographed in the mid-1850s, for example, didn't necessarily serve in the Crimea. The army at the time was meeting its usual range of demands, and challenging the Russian threat to Turkey was just one of them.

The basic organisational unit of the army was the regiment. (It still is, of course, but since our concern is the army of the past, the past tense will be used throughout, even when discussing details that still hold good today.) A regiment was made up of a number of battalions, while a brigade was a group of regiments, and a division was a group of brigades. The regular – or full-time – regiments were customarily thought of in terms of their primary fighting role: they could be categorised (in order of seniority at the outbreak of the First World War) as cavalry, foot guards, infantry and corps. Cavalry regiments were those that fought on horseback and included the Life Guards and Royal Horse Guards of the Household Cavalry along with dragoon guards, dragoons, hussars and lancers. It will be noticed that the term 'guards' allows the possibility of confusion. The guards already listed were mounted soldiers and came under the category of cavalry, whereas the second regimental grouping covered the five regiments of foot guards:

Grenadier, Scots, Coldstream, Irish and Welsh. The remaining regiments that fought on foot came under the heading of infantry. Finally, there were a number of corps and services. Each of these units offered the army as a whole its own specialised skill. These were subject to change as technologies changed, but by the end of the First World War they included corps with expertise in tanks, trench digging, signals, medicine, engineering, artillery and more besides.

To complicate matters, the regular army did not exist in isolation. It was augmented by a changing pattern of bodies known variously (and at different times) as volunteers, militia, territorials, yeomanry and reservists.

At this point, a word about horses is appropriate: a horse doesn't make a cavalryman. A photo of a soldier with a horse or (more often) wearing spurs and jodhpurs may well not depict a cavalryman. Horses were ridden by officers, regardless of regiment, and, more importantly, they were integral to military logistics up to and including the First World War. Stores, equipment and artillery had to be transported, and what couldn't be carried by the individual soldier had, for the most part, to be moved by horsepower. Many soldiers, therefore, had a mounted role and dressed accordingly, even though they were not in a cavalry regiment.

Rank insignia

Since details of uniform could depend on the rank of the wearer, and since there were changes in the way rank was shown, it can be helpful to recognise the badges of relative seniority used by the army. It should be added, though, that, here as elsewhere, a degree of generalisation is indulged in.

Officers, NCOs and privates can be seen as the rough equivalent of executives, middle managers and shop floor workers. Officers held their position by virtue of a commission from the monarch of the day. NCOs and privates were grouped together as 'other ranks' (OR), but the NCOs (non-commissioned officers) exercised authority over the private or common soldier, who was at the bottom of the hierarchy.

Officers have long been distinguished by their wearing of stars ('pips'), crowns and crossed swords. In 1902 the permutations became settled in a code that was to endure: one pip for second lieutenant; two pips for lieutenant; three pips for captain; a crown for major; a crown and one pip for lieutenant colonel; a crown and two pips for colonel; a crown and three pips for brigadier; one pip and crossed swords for major general; one crown and crossed swords for lieutenant general; one crown, one pip and crossed swords for general. It need hardly be said that the higher the rank, the less chance there is of finding an example in the family. It might be added that officers were also often distinguishable from other ranks by the superior cut and fit of their uniforms.

The refinements of NCOs' rank can be a little confusing, but the basic badge system was based on shallow chevrons (stripes) worn on the sleeve. One stripe denoted a lance corporal, two a corporal and three a sergeant. But the world of sergeants was complicated, extending to such distinctions as warrant officer and sergeant major. Some sorts of senior sergeant wore a crown above their three stripes, and others wore simply a crown or a crown enclosed in a wreath. Further confusion arises in the case of the Royal Artillery, which used a slightly different set of titles and used them in its own way. Until 1915 its NCOs, in descending order, were: sergeant (three stripes), corporal (two stripes) and bombardier (one stripe). After 1915 it dispensed with the rank of corporal, and the sequence became: sergeant (three stripes), bombardier (two stripes) and lance corporal (one stripe).

Privates bore no insignia of rank and were most numerous of all.

An overview of change

The British infantryman of the 1840s cut a striking figure. He wore, typically, a short, close-fitting jacket or coatee with a high collar and white trimmings, white trousers, white cross-belts forming an X shape across the chest, and a shako-style hat. There was minimal distinction between full (ceremonial) and service (working) dress, so – give or take the odd plume and ornament – he had to fight in much the same garb as he wore for a formal parade. The cavalry could look even more exotic, especially when a commanding officer took it into his head to enforce his own concept of dashing design. (This, in the case of Lord Cardigan's new uniforms for the 11th Hussars, occasioned comment in *The Times* about "the irrationality of their headgear" and "the incredible tightness of their cherry-coloured pants".)

But the Crimean War of 1854-6 provided a cruel demonstration of the army's shortcomings, one of which was an inability to equip and clothe its troops for harsh conditions far from home. The supply system collapsed, and soldiers ended up wearing whatever was available: even civilian garments were pressed into service, and photographs from the front show some very curious mixtures of attire.

It was impossible, after the inadequacies shown up by the Crimean campaign, to resist pressure for change, and the Indian Mutiny of 1857-8 added its own causes for concern. The end of the 1850s, therefore, brought an over-haul of army organisation and practices. The Honourable East India Company – a commercial organisation that had grown into a colonial administration complete with army – was abolished in 1858, and its functions and military resources were taken over by the state. At home fresh encouragement was given to volunteer forces, and in 1859 small local units were organised into coherent administrative groups (though their relationship with the regular army wasn't clearly formulated until 1881). As part of this movement for reform, training and logistics came under scrutiny and uniforms and equipment were modernised. There was a new emphasis on serviceability and quality, and, for the first time, government-owned factories were set up to produce uniforms and small arms.

Certain minor variations in uniform came into force in the 1870s, when collar badges and new headgear were introduced. But the next major date for change was 1881, with the introduction of the Cardwell reforms (named after Edward Cardwell, Secretary of State for War, 1868-74). Measures included pairing many infantry regiments and merging them to form single regiments of two battalions. The basic principle was that one battalion should be stationed at home and provide reinforcements for the other battalion serving overseas. Regiments of foot had previously been known by numbers – though many had titles as well – but their new names often emphasised county or regional affiliations. These regimental districts gave the army a geographical structure into which the various local militia and volunteer units could be fitted, so that each had a regiment to which it was formally linked. (Only the volunteer cavalry – the yeomanry – retained its independence.) The rationalisation of regiments naturally had its effect on uniform, bringing new developments in regimental insignia and a shift away from badges where a simple number was the dominating feature.

The typical infantryman by now looked noticeably different from his Crimean predecessor. He still generally wore a scarlet coat (though dark green was preferred for rifle regiments, and most cavalry regiments and supporting units wore blue), but it was a longer tunic rather than a short coatee, and the collar was lower and less constricting. Blue trousers had become the norm, and the old white cross belts had gone (though a single belt might be worn diagonally across the chest, and white backpack straps might be slipped over the shoulders). A helmet had replaced the shako.

The traditional red (and blue and green) tunics survived as everyday uniform until the beginning of the 20th century, though the last time they were worn on active service overseas was during the Egyptian War of 1882. The key date for change was 1902, when undress uniform – the slightly scaled-down version of the helmet and red coat formula – was replaced by Home Service Dress, a khaki uniform that was to last (with some modifications) until the eve of the Second World War.

The early years of the new century, before the beginning of the First World War, saw further organisational changes in the army. Yeomanry and volunteer regiments were brought together to form the Territorial Force; volunteer rifle regiments and corps were converted into volunteer battalions of the regular county regiments with which they had been associated; the London area volunteers were brought together to become the London Regiment; the term 'militia' was dropped in favour of Special Reserve, though it was revived in 1921. Further changes came when war broke out, as Kitchener's New Army was recruited and incorporated into the larger organisation.

By this time, and in the years that followed, the soldier was dressed for the job he had to do. In the late 1930s the battledress replaced the tunic, but the dominance of khaki remained. Service dress functioned as both ceremonial and working wear. Full dress survived, and in 1937 a new version (blue tunic and trousers, with peaked cap for all ranks) was introduced to mark the coronation of George V. But – with such notable exceptions as the Household Cavalry and the five regiments of foot guards – full dress was worn only on a gradually decreasing number of special formal occasions.

The underlying design principal for uniform had become fitness for purpose, and the days were long gone when the press could sneer at embarrassingly tight cherry-coloured pants.

Questions of colour

The spread of khaki

The adoption of khaki was not an entirely clear-cut process. Derived from an Urdu and Persian word meaning 'dust-coloured', khaki was first used in the days of the East India Company in the 1840s, and khaki uniforms were worn by some units in the 1850s at the time of the Indian Mutiny. The actual colour varied, sometimes verging on orange in the early days and only later coming closer to a brownish green. This uncertainty of tone doubtless had much to do with regiments creating their own khaki uniforms by dyeing white summer clothing with whatever apparently suitable substance was to hand. In khaki's early years, coffee, curry powder and mulberry juice were all tried by experimental dyers.

But this curious colour failed to win widespread admiration. Many thought it looked shabby, and it quickly fell from favour until being revived for the Second Afghan War of 1878-80. It was this second-generation khaki that proved to be the beginning of an irresistible trend. At first the colour was used only when serving abroad, and its spread was gradual. In 1885 the Royal Artillery put aside its blue uniforms for active service overseas and opted for khaki instead. The cavalry preserved its colourful splendour abroad until almost the end of Victoria's reign; but change came eventually, and the charge of the 21st Lancers at Omdurman in 1898 was made in khaki. The home-and-away dress code lasted until the Second Boer War (1899-1902). Then, in 1902, khaki service uniform also became the everyday working wear for peacetime duties at home. An exception was made, of course, for ceremonial occasions, and blue undress uniform was worn for manoeuvres until 1912 by the Household Cavalry and by the officers of the General Staff. But, in broad terms, the new century ushered in the age of the khaki army.

Colour in monochrome

It may seem a little unhelpful to refer to red, blue and khaki, when the photographs under consideration are monochrome. Admittedly, some old colour photographs of soldiers survive, but these were hand-tinted after they were printed. The first colour process was not marketed until 1907, and, in practical terms, colour photography did not become at all common until well after the Second World War. So any colour on early photographs was painted on after routine processing had been completed, and after the subject had left the studio. In theory, this must mean there's no absolute guarantee that the colours are authentic. In practice (given the need for customer satisfaction), the probability of accuracy is actually very high.

But the vast majority of photographs are monochrome, shading from brown or black to white or near-white. Nevertheless, it is often possible to gain a reasonable idea of the original colours. Since describing shades of brown can be rather subjective, and since the definition of grey is fairly uncontroversial, the black-to-white scale is most helpful for discussing the subject. The imagination can easily convert the idea of, say, pale grey, to a tone on the scale of umber-to-white or sepia-to-cream.

Uniformly dark tunic and trousers are likely to be blue, unless there's reason to believe the wearer belongs to a rifle regiment (in which case, dark green should be considered). An apparently dark grey tunic, worn with even darker – almost black – trousers, is probably red (and the trousers are blue). One small note of caution is needed here: very early photographic emulsions made red seem unnaturally dark and blue unnaturally pale. Though the problem was not entirely overcome until the 1880s, its potential for creating confusion seems more theoretical than real.

Uniformly mid-grey tunic and trousers are an indication of khaki. The lighter material used for hot-climate khaki clothing tends to appear as a rather paler grey. In such cases, the wearing of shorts or the presence of a tropical helmet will often confirm one's suspicions. But very pale grey uniforms are occasionally encountered in fabric that doesn't look lightweight and in styles that appear distinctly Victorian. These really are grey uniforms, and they were worn by some (but by no means all) volunteer regiments. Even more rarely, a family historian may come across a combination of mid-grey tunic and pale grey trousers. This could indicate that the subject is a member of the Camel Corps, wearing grey above and pale brown below.

All-white uniforms were Indian summer wear.

The uniform in detail

Discussion so far has been very general. But much more help with dating can be found when individual garments are considered. The caveats are predictable: some items of clothing were in use for many years, and practice often varied from regiment to regiment. So the technique for dating is to amass as many clues as possible and see what sort of dating trend emerges. Photography was given to the world with the announcement of two different processes in 1839, so the possession of photographs from as early as the 1840s is theoretically possible. Most pictures in family albums are actually of a rather later date, but, for the sake of completeness, uniform from 1840 onwards is considered. Cross-reference is made to the illustrations located near the back of the book (where they are presented and numbered in approximate chronological order, rather than the apparently haphazard order they are referred to in the text).

Upper body

The waist-length and tailed coatee of the 1840s soldier was at the end of its life, and events in the Crimea forced the recognition that it was too tight for vigorous activity. It was therefore replaced in 1855 by the tunic (or, in some cases and for some occasions, by the short, close-fitting but tailless shell jacket). The tunic was a rather longer garment that reached the hip or upper thigh – and this style of jacket survived until the late 1930s. Some of the very early tunics were double-breasted, but their currency was brief and they can be dated to the second half of the 1850s. There was also a taste for contrasting trimmings on the lower sleeve from the late 1860s until the beginning of the 1880s (Figure 6). This design created an inverted V-shape at the cuff and should not be confused with rank chevrons, with the ornate braided knots that contributed to the elaborate decoration of cavalry jackets, or with the fancy braid trimming that appeared on officers' cuffs from the late 1860s (of which more in the next chapter). There was also a revival of this contrasting detail on some uniforms in the early years of the 20th century, but other details in a photograph should make it clear whether an image dates from 1875, say, or 1901. From 1902 onwards, the khaki tunic was the workaday norm (Figure 12).

The arrival of the tunic, incidentally, is less precisely datable in India, where, made of white drill, it was worn for hot weather training in the days of the East India Company and subsequently became official summer full dress.

For many years tunics were worn buttoned to the throat. Only in 1912 did it become permissible for an officer to wear an open-collared tunic with lapels, like those on a civilian suit (Figure 16). The transition to this style was not instantaneous, so whilst a glimpse of shirt and tie gives 1912 as the earliest possible year, fully buttoned-up officers can belong to a slightly later date. The collarless shirts of other ranks continued for decades to be hidden by the high-buttoned jackets, but at least in the years after 1918 their tunics had a more svelte and tailored look. During the war the army had needed to clothe a huge number of men as best it could. After 1918 the pressure was off, and more attention could be paid to the smartness of the ordinary soldier.

There was one notable exception to the principle of the unseen shirt, and that came about in the late 1930s, when men serving in the Middle East were allowed to wear khaki drill shirts with rolled-up sleeves and open collars. This practice continued in warmer locations during the Second World War (Figure 20).

In March 1939 the demise of the tunic was announced. It was to be replaced by a waist length blouse, which buttoned at the cuffs, and which was part of the newly designed 'battle suit'. Though short in the body, this battledress blouse was more generously cut than the coatees and shell jackets of the previous century. But, for the common soldier, it still buttoned up at the throat (Figure 19). It naturally took a little time to re-clothe the army, especially since numbers were growing with the outbreak of a new war. But the majority of soldiers were wearing the new design within a year, and photographs of soldiers in tunics in 1940, though possible, are not common.

At last, in September 1944, other ranks were permitted to wear their blouse open-necked, with shirt collar and tie showing, when off duty. From 1947 this look became acceptable, but not universal, on duty. In practice, however, the distribution of collared shirts was slow, and many soldiers still had the collarless version until 1949. Not until the 1950s did the open-necked tunic become standard wear. One final refinement of the tunic was a lapel buttonhole. If that can be discerned in a photo, it's an indication the picture was taken in 1949 or later.

Grey greatcoats, which look fairly pale in monochrome pictures, enjoyed some favour in the middle of the 19th century. But after 1868 only the regiments of guards wore them. So, on a known non-guard of Victorian times, such a coat has a latest possible date. In the next century the khaki uniform had its own greatcoat. This quickly proved unsuitable for conditions in the muddy trenches of the First World War. But cold still caused much discomfort, and in the early years of the war many soldiers acquired jackets of fur or shaggy goatskin to keep them warm. Eventually, as an official solution to the problem, the troops were issued with sleeveless jerkins of leather, lined with wool. So a leather garment points to 1916 or later, while the fiercely unkempt look is more likely to date from 1916 or earlier. (Caution is necessary, however, as the soldiers were in no hurry to abandon the cosiness of their hairy body-warmers.)

Lower body

In 1845 blue trousers replaced the trousers of white duck that the infantry wore for home service. Thereafter, white trousers were generally reserved for service in India and for bandsmen. The cavalry's famously tight trousers of earlier years were superseded after the Crimean War by 'booted overalls' – rather looser garments worn with boots. These, in their turn, gave way in 1871 to pantaloons with knee-high boots, and this rather dressy style was maintained overseas by the cavalry as well as at home.

For infantrymen the 1870s saw the emergence of puttees (the Hindustani word for bandages). These long strips of cloth, which were wound around the lower leg, did indeed produce a bandaged look. They were first seen during the Second Afghan War (1878-80) and were subsequently worn in the Sudan during the 1880s. They went on to become a standard feature of khaki uniform (Figure 14) and survived until the end of the 1930s. Their full incorporation into the khaki field service uniform was not, however, immediate, and from 1902 until around 1907 short black leather leggings made a brief appearance (Figure 11).

From 1902, when khaki trousers accompanied the new khaki tunics, a distinction between mounted and unmounted troops became evident. Instead of ordinary trousers, soldiers who rode horses wore garments suited to their role. For other ranks this often meant reinforced breeches (the tougher inside legs of which are usually quite discernible in photographs), while for officers it generally meant jodhpurs (the generous hip-level cut of which is readily noticeable). Various kinds of leather boots and lace-up protectors encased the lower legs of officers, while the ensemble of other ranks was more likely to be completed by puttees (which were sometimes wound from knee to ankle by mounted soldiers, rather than from ankle to knee, as practised by others). Any of these lower-leg styles might be set off with the addition of spurs. (Figure 16 shows officers and senior NCOs in an interesting variety of legwear.) Remember, incidentally, that a mounted soldier was not necessarily a cavalryman: the vast majority of army transport was horse-drawn, and all officers – whatever their regiment – were expected to be able to ride.

Many Scottish regiments were kilted, and a khaki apron was often worn over the kilt during the First World War. So a plain apron of a single colour dates a picture to 1914 or after.

Shorts were added to the military wardrobe a little earlier than might, perhaps, be expected. They were worn by some troops during the First World War in such locations as Mesopotamia and Palestine. But they became more common for overseas postings between the wars and, along with trousers of lightweight drill, were standard issue for hot climates from the late 1930s onward (Figure 20).

Puttees (even with shorts) survived until 1939, when the battledress uniform was introduced. They were then replaced by short webbing gaiters, which were strapped around the ankles. Whereas puttees had risen almost to the knee, gaiters simply caught up the bottoms of the trouser legs. The loose lower-leg fabric was then folded down, more or less smartly, over the tops of the gaiters (Figure 19).

Headgear

Hats can prove particularly helpful for dating. They were sometimes removed for studio portraits, but on such occasions they were frequently placed in full view beside the soldier on a piece of studio furniture.

Whilst practice varied, and whilst highland regiments formed a notable exception, the infantry's most common form of headdress until the late 1870s was the shako – a tall, near-cylindrical hat. Style succeeded style with some frequency, but the version in favour in photography's earliest days was the bell-topped shako. The top of this flared out, as its name suggests, like the rim of a bell. Lofty, black and leather-peaked, its badge was set high at the front and was surmounted by a small fluffy orb known as a ball tuft (a detail that went on to feature on every subsequent model of shako).

Then, in 1845, the Albert shako was introduced. Named after the Prince Consort and familiarly referred to as 'the Albert pot', this headdress had a front peak and virtually parallel sides. (In fact, there was a very slight flare to the officers' version, but none at all in the case of other ranks.) At the back was a second smaller peak, which is not generally evident in photographs unless it is seen from the side. But the resemblance to a black chimney pot is diagnostic and the height is very apparent. If you imagine a line drawn from the top of the shako's crown to tip of the wearer's chin, the rim of the hat comes at the halfway point, with the front peak projecting lower still.

Whilst the Albert shako looked impressive on parade, it proved cumbersome in the Crimea, and in 1856 the French pattern shako replaced it. This new design, though still tall, was noticeably shorter than its predecessor. It, too, was black with two peaks – the larger at the front and the smaller at the rear. But it was a little higher at the back than the front, and this gave it the appearance of being slightly tapered and tilted forward. It lasted only a few years before being succeeded in 1862 by the quilted shako. This also had a sloping, tapered look, but it had no rear peak and it was considerably lower than the French pattern. In fact, the crown was about 4 inches (10cm) high at the front and 6½ inches (16.5 cm) high at the back. The quilting was on the crown of the officers' version, which was covered in dark blue cloth; but the blue was so dark that it's indistinguishable from black in photographs, and the stitching is unlikely to show. The reduced height is what catches the attention, and to the modern eye this is probably the first shako to look like mildly practical headgear rather than fancy dress. It was in use until the end of the decade.

The last shako belonged to the years 1870-78 (Figure 3). In shape and colour it was very like the quilted shako, but it differed in a number of ways from earlier styles. The officers' version had two strips of gold braid around the top of the crown. Like earlier shakos, it had a leather chinstrap, but this leather strap served as a backing for a chain of brass rings. In addition, its badge looked different. A shako's regimental badge was set in a much larger decorative badge plate, which until this time had normally taken the form of an eight-pointed star, surmounted by a crown. But the last shako surrounded its badge by a metal plate shaped like a crown-topped wreath. Even when details of the badge itself are indecipherable, it is often possible to decide whether the enclosing design is shaped like a star or like a wreath. This last version of the shako was worn by Royal Marines, militia, corps and most infantry regiments, but not by rifle and fusilier regiments or by many Scottish regiments. Ironically, sporadic revivals of the shako in later years included its adoption by some rifle regiments in the 1890s and the Highland Light Infantry in the early 20th century. By the late 1870s, however, the shako had reached the end of its long run as dominant military style.

Its replacement was the cloth helmet, which was introduced in 1878. There had been very limited trials of its suitability in the preceding year or two, after which the helmet became standard and almost universal wear for the infantry and corps. (There were isolated pockets of shako wearing until 1881.) The new helmet was made of cork and covered in blue cloth, and it was tall and rose to a dome. Infantry regiments wore it with a pointed spike on top (Figure 8), while the corps and supporting services had a ball-topped version (Figure 7). In the case of the Royal Artillery it's necessary to be a little more precise: RA helmets bore a spike until 1881 and a ball thereafter. The cork helmet continued in use until 1914, though in its later years it was just one of a variety of possible forms of headgear.

Helmets were also designed for hot climates. A sun helmet was issued to all ranks of the Artillery in India in 1858, at the time when the East India Company's forces were incorporated into the national army. Then, in 1877, a white sun helmet was authorised for all soldiers on service overseas (Figure 8). This, like the home service helmet, was a tall dome made of cloth-covered cork. It was a little longer at the back (about 12 inches or 30 cm) than the front (about 10¾ inches or 27 cm). Sometimes a khaki cover was fitted over it, and sometimes a neck-flap was affixed behind to give protection against the sun. Its use continued until the opening years of the 20th century, but it was not the only kind of helmet to find favour overseas.

The Wolsley helmet – named after Sir James Garnet Wolsley, commander-in-chief during the Egyptian War of 1882 – had some initial use in overseas campaigns at the end of the 19th century and became standard tropical wear in 1902. Made of cork and covered in pale khaki, it had a markedly lower crown than the white helmet, though its top was still rounded (Figure 11). Wound about it and covering the lower half of the crown was a pagri, or puggaree. This lightweight scarf (its name a borrowing from Hindi) was intended to give extra protection against the sun. Instead of bearing a metal regimental badge at the front, the Wolsley helmet had a cloth badge attached to the pagri at the side. It continued in use in India until 1938, when it was replaced by a lightweight pith helmet. That, at least, is the theory. In practice there is some confusion of both definitions and dates to contend with.

The term 'sola topi' has so far been avoided, not least because the Wolsley helmet wasn't one. A brief etymological diversion is necessary. A topi is a hat (Hindi); sola (Urdu and Bengali) or shola (Hindi) is spongewood – a plant related to gorse, laburnum and pea. The pith of sola can be used to make lightweight hats. So 'sola topi' and 'pith helmet' are essentially the same thing. ('Solar topi' is a very natural mistake, based on an assumption that the name derives from the hat's purpose rather than its construction.) So, despite being sometimes inaccurately described as such, the cork-based Wolsley helmet was not really a sola topi. But for some years it coexisted with the genuine article.

The date of the pith helmet's introduction is not clear. Officially it became standard wear in India in 1938, when it supplanted the cork headgear. It had a rather flat top, which gave a squarish look to the crown; it had no pagri; and it had a quilted khaki cover, the diamond-patterned stitching of which can be made out in photos of reasonably good quality. But it's clear that this sola helmet had already been in use for some time before the 1930s, and photographic evidence suggests that it was being worn as early as 1917 (Figure 15). Nor did the supplanting go entirely to plan. Wolsley helmets survived side by side with pith helmets for a year or two, and a few were still being worn in some Middle East locations as late as 1948. Dating photographs by sun helmets should therefore be a matter of considering broad trends rather than relying on exact dates.

One other kind of helmet has yet to be considered. The steel (or Brodie) helmet, was first issued for use in the trenches in October 1915, was widespread by early 1916, and was often referred to by soldiers as the 'battle bowler'. Its presence in a photograph is an indication that the picture was taken near the front. Regimental badges were sometimes attached in the early days. This practice was stopped in late 1917, however, on the grounds that drilling holes to affix the badge would weaken the helmet.

But reinforced headgear was not the only kind that saw service in the army, and to start examining the various kinds of softer hat, it's necessary to go back a few years.

The pillbox cap was a low, straight-sided hat with no peak (Figure 6). It was, in essence, a very short tube with a lid on, and it was generally worn tilted a little to one side. Cavalry officers and infantry other ranks wore it on occasions during the second half of the 19th century. It had generally fallen out of favour by the late 1890s, though some cavalry and artillery use continued until about 1903. The forage cap, or patrol cap, was a pillbox with an added peak. Originally adopted by some cavalry units, this cap became quite common across the army for undress wear by the mid-19th century. It, too, had become largely obsolete by the century's end.

The busby has first to be defined. In colloquial usage the term is often applied to the high round-topped bearskin cap of the guards. More properly, however, the busby is a slightly less tall fur hat, with a bag hanging down to the right and a plume on the top at the front. (The end of the bag could originally be attached to the right shoulder as a defence against sabre cuts.) It was worn primarily by the cavalry – specifically by hussar regiments – and its longevity makes it fairly unhelpful for dating purposes. But there is an exception. Between 1855 and 1878 the busby was adopted by the Royal Artillery and the Royal Engineers, and they wore it with a difference: their busbies usually had the plume attached to the left side (Figure 2). Apart from the position of their plumes, busbied non-hussars can also often be identified by white belts and by the relatively modest amount of frogging on their jackets. Though the RA and RE both generally went over to helmets in 1878, the busby survived in one branch of the RA – the Royal Horse Artillery – into the early years of the 20th century. Worn with rather dashing shell jackets, these RHA busbies could easily be misleading, were it not for the fact that their plumes were still set on the side.

The Glengarry cap, a new undress cap for the infantry and some corps, was introduced in 1874. It was a narrow peakless cap running from front to back of the head. A crease along its top created a double ridge; its badge was fastened to the side; and it had ribbons hanging down behind (where they often eluded the camera's gaze). It continued in widespread use into the 1880s, after which time it became exclusive to Scottish regiments. In many cases, a Scottish Glengarry cap can be recognised by the addition of a chequered band around its base (Figure 5). So an unchequered Glengarry probably (but not certainly) belongs to the 1870s or 1880s, while a chequered example could date from as late as the 20th century.

The khaki slouch hat or bush hat – a broad-brimmed soft hat with the left side of the brim folded up – was based on headgear worn by the Australian armed forces, and it became popular with the British army (and with mounted troops especially) during the Second Boer War of 1899-1901. It was then briefly tried for home wear in 1902-3, but this experiment was quickly discontinued. Thereafter it was worn only in West Africa until 1943, when it became widespread among troops in the Far East.

The Broderick forage cap – named after the Secretary of State for War – was never popular. Introduced in 1902 or 1903 (sources differ), it was a dark blue, peakless cap that was wider at the top than at the base (Figure 10). The basic shape was that of a pillbox cap with a flat plate of slightly greater diameter on top. Alternatively, it can be thought of as resembling the field service cap described in the next paragraph, but with the peak amputated. Soldiers hated it, because they thought it too German in appearance. In an attempt to reduce its offensiveness, a peaked khaki cover was produced to fit over it, and this was sometimes worn in 1904 and 1905. In photographs, its khaki tone may not quite match that of the rest of the uniform and the softness of its fabric peak is evident. By 1906 the Broderick cap was, for most troops, a thing of the past, though its very few later wearers did include some ranks of the Royal Marines until the time of the First World War.

The peaked service cap (often known simply as the service cap) proved more tenacious. It was a low, round, peaked khaki cap, and the top of its crown (which, as with the Broderick cap, was of greater circumference than the base) was held flat and rigid by a stiffener (Figure 12). It's the hat that is seen in so many pictures from the First World War. Indeed, the majority of photographed examples date from those years, but the cap itself lasted from the beginning of the 20th century until it the eve of the Second World War and, for some wearers, beyond. The basic shape was not entirely new: a baggier version had been worn by some officers in the 1850s. But in its khaki version it was part of the sweeping changes of 1902. At first it was worn by infantry officers, but cavalry regiments and infantry other ranks quickly followed, and by 1905 the peaked service cap had been widely adopted as the usual undress headgear.

During the First World War, soldiers at the front line frequently removed the stiffeners from their caps to soften their silhouette and to make them less obvious to snipers (Figure 17). This practice was a technical infringement of regulations, but it clearly went largely unchecked, since photographs show that officers and NCOs as well as privates customised their hats (Figure 16). A picture of a soldier in a battered peaked cap is, therefore, a picture of a soldier who has seen service in the trenches. The jauntiness with which these misshapen items are sometimes worn in studio portraits perhaps suggests a satisfied awareness of rules being bent with impunity. In 1917 a soft and foldable version of the peaked cap appeared. Recognisable by the close parallel rows of stitching across the peak, these hats survived alongside the standard version (for active service and manoeuvres) until 1933.

Once hostilities ended, the stiffeners were replaced and the service dress cap remained standard wear for all ranks in most regiments in the years between the wars. Then, in 1939, came a change to the folding field service cap. This was intended to apply to all ranks, but many officers contrived to continue wearing their peaked caps during the Second World War. After the war the peaked cap was reinstated for officers and for certain senior NCOs.

The folding field service cap, or side cap, was essentially a shallow envelope of fabric that opened to run from front to back of the head and that was worn tilted to the right (Figure 19). Whilst not dissimilar in effect to the Glengarry, it was less artfully shaped and it had no ribbons. Its soft fabric and simple shape meant it could be folded lengthwise and tucked under a shoulder strap when not being worn (Figure 18). The side cap had been in army use since around 1870, but only in 1933 did it become – in its khaki incarnation – sufficiently widespread to allow generalisations about dating. Initially it was brought in to replace the soft, stitched version of the peaked cap, but shortly after, in March 1939, it became the regulation headdress for most of the army. From 1940 it became permissible when off duty, to replace the khaki side cap with one in regimental colours (Figure 20). This helps with dating any picture of a soldier in battledress whose side cap is of an obviously different tone.

Unfortunately the side cap presented problems: it was hard to settle at the right angle; it gave no protection against either sun or rain; it blew away in a strong wind; it fell off during vigorous activity. It also absorbed the greasy hair preparations of the Brylcreem Age in a way that its shape did nothing to disguise. It was therefore replaced by a beret, which was pulled down to the right side of the head. The Tank Corps had already started to wear a black beret in 1930, and in 1941 the entire Royal Armoured Corps (which included some cavalry and infantry regiments as well as tank personnel) moved over to the new headgear. In 1942 the newly formed Airborne Forces adopted maroon berets, and in 1942 khaki berets were authorised for a wide range of regiments. The complete transition took a little while, for wartime presented no shortage of pressing matters to attend to. So group photos showing a mixture of side caps and berets are not unknown (Figure 20), and pictures show that the Home Guard was never in the vanguard of sartorial change (Figure 19). But by 1943 the full-time army was a predominantly bereted force.

Accoutrements in detail

There is more to uniform than its basic garments, and dating clues can be provided by a wide range of embellishments and items of equipment. These are all grouped under the heading 'accoutrements', which is a military term, but which is used a little improperly here to include some items that fall outside the strict military definition. Treatment of individual themes is often rather fragmentary, since the aim is less to provide a history of accoutrements than to pick out some pertinent details that can be recognised with relative ease.

Hat badges

The common preoccupation of family historians, when faced with a cap badge, is to identify the regiment. That is not the concern of the present work, but a number of helpful books on the subject are mentioned in the bibliography. (It's a vast area, and one of the volumes listed contains over 1800 illustrations.) There are, however, occasional dating clues to be gleaned from headdress badges.

The cloth helmet (like the shako) had its badge set in a decorative metal plate. For most regiments this took the form of a wreath set against the shape of an eight-pointed star, with the top point of the star obscured by a crown (Figure 8). The star's points were a little longer and sharper in the officers' version. The design of the surmounting crown was changed when Queen Victoria died. The Victorian crown, used on helmet plates from 1878 to 1901, was basically St Edward's Crown: it bulged out at the sides to create a shape suggesting the front half of a butterfly. From 1902 to 1914, in the time of Edward VII and George V, a design based on the Imperial Crown was used: the upper part came up in a smooth curve to the apex, resulting in an outline reminiscent of a fairy cake with a nicely risen top. This difference between crowns also applies to such stand-alone cap badges as featured them, and a crown's silhouette can often be picked out in photographs, even when details of the regimental badge are unclear.

The stand-alone cap badge, without any backing plate, was more suitable for the smaller and softer varieties of headdress, and examples (sometimes embroidered) can be seen on pillboxes and forage caps. But the significant boost to the freestanding badge came with the introduction of the Glengarry in 1874, and the modern variety of regimental symbol has its roots in the Cardwell reforms of 1881. Before that date numerical badges were common for infantry regiments (Figure 4); after that date a number was occasionally incorporated into a badge, but the overall emphasis was on emblematic design. A simple numerical cap badge, therefore, gives a latest possible date (as well, of course, as identifying the pre-Cardwell regiment). Rank insignia were very occasionally worn on headgear, and their significance is discussed in the next section. Cap badges for the cavalry, incidentally, were not introduced until 1894.

Discussion of individual regimental badges has so far been carefully avoided. It might be appropriate, however, to make an exception in the case of the Royal Artillery, since its badge is encountered with unusual frequency. The reason for this is simple: the Artillery was a huge organisation. Made up of three separate bodies – the Royal Garrison Artillery, the Royal Field Artillery and the Royal Horse Artillery – it had a maximum strength in the First World War of nearly 549,000 men. Where many regiments sustained casualties in thousands, the RA sustained tens of thousands. Even such huge corps as the Royal Engineers (maximum strength over 237,000) and the Labour Corps (over 389,000) appear small in comparison. It's little wonder, then, that RA cap badges figure so frequently in photographs.

The RA badge of a field gun was adopted in 1902. With a crown above the gun and a scroll below, it has a characteristically triangular appearance. The gun's rather thin left-hand strut is, however, sometimes hard to pick out in photos, and this can create the illusion of a somewhat unbalanced look. The spaces between the spokes of the gun's large wheel were normally cut away, allowing the darker background of the headdress to show through. But economy versions of some regiments' badges were produced during the First World War, and in the case of the RA this meant that, from 1916 to 1918, new badges were left unpierced.

Rank insignia

During the era of the (usually) red tunic, there were changes in the ways in which officers' uniforms proclaimed their ranks to the world. From 1855 until 1880 the appropriate permutation of stars and/or crowns was worn on the collar (Figure 3). Then, in October 1880, the order was given for these motifs to be moved to the shoulder cord, and this system continued until 1902. But, in addition to these collar- or shoulder-borne insignia, officers wore rank-related decoration on the lower sleeve. From 1855 to 1868 this took the form of a panel, which contained the relevant star/crown combination, and which was outlined by one or more borders of lace braid (Figure 1). In 1868 the panels were replaced by deep inverted lace chevrons on the cuff (Figure 3). These had slightly curved lines and, often, a small stylised knot at the point. The thicker and more ornate was the lace, the higher was the rank. If comparisons are of any help, then the lines of a stylised Christmas tree or the shape of a slightly opened umbrella come to mind.

This sequence of changes created a series of datable combinations. Collar plus panel indicates 1855-68; collar plus lace chevrons equals 1868-80; shoulder plus lace chevrons means 1880-1902. (It may not always be easy to make out the shoulder insignia against the background of the shoulder cord, but the absence of insignia from the collar is generally clear enough and carries its own implications.)

The next major development came in November 1902, when the introduction of khaki service dress brought with it a new system of showing rank. (Though this was almost universal, certain Scottish uniforms were excepted, and the change was not adopted for officers of the Brigade of Guards.) The system involved a return to pips and crowns on cuff panels, but since these were now generally being worn with khaki uniforms, confusion with the earlier style is not very likely. The new panel took the form of a false flap outlined in braid, and additional hoops of braid were sewn around the cuff to join the flap at its central point (Figure 16). The effect, at first glance, is as if the panel has been tied on by the strip (or strips) of lace braid.

One other datable detail arises from the 1902 changes. In earlier years, one star had been used to denote a lieutenant and two stars had signified a captain. But in 1902 a single star was made the badge of the second lieutenant. This had a knock-on effect, with two stars for a lieutenant and three for a captain. So a three-pip officer cannot date from earlier than 1902.

In theory, the officers' cuff rank markings lasted until their abolition in 1920, when the pips and stars migrated back to the shoulder. In practice, shoulder pips on khaki uniforms can date from as early as 1915. This overlap resulted from the practicalities of life in the trenches. Fairly early on in the First World War some officers moved their insignia to their shoulder straps. This, they believed, made them less immediately recognisable as targets than did the eye-catching panels. The practice initially met with official disapproval, but in 1917 the practicality of the infringement was accepted, and officers were allowed to choose for themselves whether to wear rank insignia on the sleeve or on the shoulder. After the war, in 1920, cuff badges were abandoned completely.

Less help is given by the rank insignia of NCOs, whose system of sleeve chevrons dates back to the very early 19th century. But a few clues are possible at the most senior NCO levels. The actual rank titles – quartermaster sergeants, company and regimental sergeant majors, and warrant officers of various classes – can be confusing, but their stripes and badges are to a degree datable. In 1802 the army introduced the wearing of four stripes or chevrons by certain senior sergeants, and this lasted until 1871, when a crown was added above the stripes. In 1882 the chevrons were all removed, leaving just a crown on the lower sleeve to indicate the wearer's rank. In 1901 some warrant officers acquired a wreath to enclose their crown, and from 1915 onwards most of them wore badges depicting the Royal Arms.

In theory, it would appear helpful to note whether an NCO wears his stripes on one sleeve or both, but regimental variations in practice cloud the issue. In 1881, for instance, the order went out that NCOs' chevrons should be worn on the right arm only. But it's a mistake to assume that NCOs using both sleeves had previously been the norm. The NCOs of the light infantry and fusiliers had indeed been wearing their rank insignia on both arms, but many regiments had already been following the single-arm system.

A very few regiments made use of rank chevrons on pillbox caps. Where they were worn, they generally continued in use as long as the cap itself, but there is one exception. Cap chevrons were mainly confined to the junior levels of NCO; their use for sergeants was rare, and three-stripe hat badges appear not to have been worn after 1864.

Other arm and shoulder badges

Whilst regimental badges were sometimes worn on the sleeve, practice varied from regiment to regiment. As a very broad generalisation, it can be said that they were worn mostly by senior NCOs and that more were worn in cavalry regiments than elsewhere. But, if the specific regiment is not known, they seem unlikely to help with dating. There was, however, a range of other sleeve and shoulder insignia that can sometimes prove useful.

'Shoulder titles' is a term covering regimental identification badges worn on shoulder straps (Figure 5), shoulder cords or, sometimes, the very top of the sleeve. They were first worn in 1881 on the tropical uniform of officers in India. Within three or four years their use was taken up for other ranks and for other locations, but they were not really widespread until about 1908. They were not always issued, however, to soldiers in the First World War. The absence of a shoulder title does not therefore prove a pre-1881 date; but the presence of one does indicate 1881 or later.

The shoulder straps of khaki tunics underwent an evolutionary process in their early years. The shoulder strap of 1902-04 was detachable. It had a central stripe running along its length, and it may appear in photos to be of a slightly different tone from the tunic on which it sits. From about 1904 to 1907 a strip of braided cord was used instead. Finally, in 1907, came the fully attached strap that was a fixed part of the garment and made from the same fabric as the rest of it (Figure 11).

There is a history of using cloth arm badges to denote particular appointments. A sleeve badge for bandsmen of all ranks was introduced in 1907. This featured a lyre, set between sprigs of laurel and surmounted by a crown. From 1907 to 1952 the crown was of the Imperial (or round-topped) variety; in 1953 it was changed to the St Edward's crown, as used in the reign of Queen Victoria.

A wide range of other badges was used to mark out trade proficiency or skill-at-arms, and many of these were introduced in the 1890s. (Some can be recognised by an X-shaped motif: crossed flags for a signaller, for example, crossed axes for a pioneer, and crossed field-gun barrels for artillery proficiency.) Until the beginning of the First World War, these badges were worn on the left forearm, but from about 1914 onward they were sewn to the right sleeve. Some of the badges had a fairly short life: the fleur-de-lys symbol of the army scout was adopted at the end of the 19th century and was not worn after 1918. But others lasted longer than might be expected. The crossed whips of the army driver, introduced by 1898, outlived the age of the horse and survived until the Second World War.

During the First World War, from mid-1915 on, there was also some use of cloth badges, worn high on the sleeve, to aid the identification of troops in the field. Though there were some fairly ambitious designs, most of these badges were relatively simple and took the form of basic geometrical shapes – coloured diamonds, circles, squares and the like. These badges became redundant once the war was over.

Three other arm badges are particularly common in pictures from the First World War, though the first of them was actually introduced over a quarter of a century earlier. Good conduct chevrons were authorised in 1881, and they are also sometimes referred to as long service stripes. In practice, they fulfilled both functions. They were shallow chevrons of the same size as NCOs' rank chevrons, but they were sewn on with the point facing upwards (Figure 17). Soldiers under the rank of corporal who met the appropriate criteria could wear them on the left forearm. A man qualified for one such stripe after two years' service, provided that his name hadn't appeared in the Regimental Conduct Book during that period. A second stripe was awarded after six years and a third after twelve. A fourth stripe, awarded after 18 years' offence-free service, was possible, but the required length of time, sustained virtue and lack of promotion would have combined to make it an unusual distinction. (In counting stripes, incidentally, count simply the pale chevrons and ignore the strips of braid that separate them.)

Apart from providing a 'not-before' date, these service stripes generally help with dating only if it's known when a soldier joined up. The significant exception comes at the time of the First World War, when an ancestor is known to have been a wartime soldier rather than a long-term regular. Then, although the exact date of enlistment may not be known, it's clear that even the promptest volunteer couldn't have qualified for a good conduct stripe before 1916.

The second arm badge often seen in photographs from the Great War is the overseas service chevron. This was markedly smaller than the rank and good conduct chevron and it was worn, point upwards, on the right arm just above the cuff (Figure 17). These chevrons recorded service overseas from 4th August 1914 onwards. The first chevron marked the occasion of a soldier's departure from home, and a new one was then earned by each unbroken period of twelve months outside the UK. (Periods of leave of less than a month were overlooked when doing the calculations.) But the overseas service stripes were not actually introduced until December 1917, when they were awarded retrospectively. So, as a dating aid, they indicate that a picture was taken in (realistically) 1918 or later, as well as providing some supplementary information about the soldier's service. The qualifying period for earning the chevrons ended on 1st May 1920, and their wearing was discontinued in 1922.

The third frequent First World War arm badge is the wound stripe. These stripes were short straight bars, coloured gold, and worn vertically on the line from wrist to elbow (Figure 13). The lower end was set about three inches from the bottom of the left sleeve, and if more than one was earned, the stripes were set parallel to each other. They were introduced in July 1916 and, where appropriate, were awarded retrospectively. The key criterion was being recorded as 'wounded' on an official casualty list, and gas victims and the shell-shocked did not qualify. Wound stripes were discontinued in 1922.

In the Second World War the use of cloth upper sleeve badges was revived for use in the field, but in 1943 a new kind of badge was introduced. This took the form of a cloth arc. It identified the wearer's regiment, and it was sewn to the very top of the sleeve, right next to the shoulder seam. (Some similar badges had been used on the old khaki tunics as early as 1902, but a cloth arc of this kind on a battledress blouse belongs to 1943 or later.)

There was also a return, late on in the Second World War, to issuing wound stripes and overseas service stripes. As before, the wound stripes took the form of short upright bars on the left sleeve, and the overseas service stripes were small inverted chevrons worn on the right forearm. Both kinds of stripe were authorised in February 1944. Their appearance in photos is rare, however. Distribution was slow, and soldiers entitled to wear the stripes were often demobilised before receiving them.

Buttons and collar badges

Collar badges offer only minimal help with dating. Metal versions were introduced for the other ranks of almost all infantry regiments in 1874, and they began to be added to officers' uniforms from 1881 onwards. The presence of a metal collar badge does, therefore, give an earliest possible date. But its absence is not necessarily informative, for there were exceptions. There were regiments of guards that already wore embroidered cloth collar badges and continued to do so; and neither the King's Royal Rifle Corps (the 60th Regiment of Foot until 1881) nor the Rifle Brigade adopted the new badges. In addition, collar badges were not always issued to other ranks during the First World War. Collar badges were adopted rather later by the cavalry. The first, seen in the mid-1890s, were the Roman numerals worn by hussars on the collars of undress tunics. They were more common from 1902 onwards, but even by 1914 the collar badge was not universal cavalry wear.

Buttons tend to be equally uncommunicative, especially since their details can be hard to make out in photographs. Until the early 1870s brass regimental buttons were the infantry norm, and after that time general service buttons displaying the royal arms were used for other ranks and junior NCOs. But it takes a sharp photo for the difference to be confidently picked out. Brass buttons were discontinued in 1939, though it took about a year for the change to other materials (and, sometimes, concealed buttons) to be completed. Since this development coincided with the shift from tunic to battledress blouse, it only confirms a dating judgement that can be made on other grounds.

Items worn on the chest

A full treatment of medals is not attempted here. They can be difficult to identify in photographs and they were often authorised – and even more often worn – well after the event. So only very few examples have been selected.

If a medal in the shape of a five-pointed star is worn by an obviously Victorian soldier, it's worth considering whether it could be the Khedive's Star. Awarded in the 1880s (from 1882 onward), this decoration could only be worn together with the round Egypt Medal, which bore an image of the sphinx. Even if details are hard to make out on a photo, the combination of the two shapes side-by-side is at least suggestive of an interpretation and decade (Figure 6).

Dating from the First World War, the 1914 Star and the 1914-15 Star have a shared and distinctive shape. Though they are eight-pointed stars, their points alternate in sharpness between about 60° (at top, bottom and sides) and about 15° (set between the wider angles). This is because the design is made up of a diamond shape (with slightly concave sides) that serves as a background to crossed swords, the tips and hilts of which supply the remaining four points. A crown sits on the topmost point. The two medals would look the same in most photos, and their earliest possible date is 1917.

If it proves possible to read the figures on a medal, it may be helpful to know that the 1914 Star was authorised in 1917, and the 1914-1915 Star came into being in 1919.

A badge that is sometimes seen on a soldier's chest from 1912 onward is the Imperial Service Tablet. This is a narrow metal oblong, in landscape format, with a crown set at the centre of its long top edge. Territorial soldiers who volunteered for overseas duties, which they were not at that time obliged to take up, wore it on the right breast.

One other item sometimes worn on the chest was the sash. From 1768 until 1855 infantry officers wore a sash around the waist, but from 1855 until 1902 the officer's sash passed across the chest via the left shoulder (Figure 1). In 1902 sashes, when worn, returned to the waist. Sergeants, too, wore sashes around the waist before 1855. After that date, however, those entitled to wear a sash wore it over the right shoulder (Figure 9), thereby avoiding confusion with officers.

Facial hair

Whilst its inclusion as an accoutrement is perhaps stretching the meaning, facial hair may prove helpful – at least as supporting evidence – when the date of a photograph is being considered.

Beards and luxuriant side-whiskers were often worn by soldiers in the 1850s, 1860s and – to a lesser degree – 1870s (Figure 4). But beards don't seem to have been particularly favoured in later years, except for two brief periods: they had a spell of popularity in South Africa in the Second Boer War of 1899-1902; and they were grown by desert patrols and by General Orde Wingate's commando force in Burma during the Second World War.

Moustaches had their devotees throughout the decades, but never more than in the opening years of the 20th century (Figure 11). In the early 1900s it was customary to leave the upper lip unshaven and produce a vigorous moustache. (Options included the bushy 'walrus' style subsequently immortalised in Bruce Bairnsfather's 'Old Bill' cartoons). The practice was still widespread at the beginning of the First World War, when huge numbers of bare-lipped recruits joined the bristling regulars. Many of the newcomers fell in with the moustache-growing tradition, but their taste was often for something smaller and more carefully cultivated. The results did not impress the authorities, and in due course the order went out that 'unsoldierly' moustaches were not acceptable: a soldier must either grow a full and manly moustache or refrain from growing a moustache at all. Given the choice of all or nothing, many men settled for nothing, and since the First World War the majority of soldiers have been clean-shaven.

All this has possible implications for dating photos apparently taken between 1900 and 1920, but conclusions must be drawn tentatively. There were clean-shaven soldiers before the Great War, so facial hair – or the lack of it – must not be relied on to date a picture of just one of two soldiers. But speculation about such matters becomes legitimate when examining group photos, and the larger the group, the more likely it becomes that a probability can be proposed. A group with a very high incidence of heavy moustaches (and only heavy moustaches) is likely to be from the pre-war years of the 20th century or from the very beginning of the war. A group where a significant number of small moustaches are mixed in among the bushier variety could well belong to the early years of the First World War. A group where most upper lips are shaved but a few carry assertive moustaches is likely to date from the war's middle or later years (Figure 16).

Belts, bags and straps

The infantry's broad white cross-belts were abolished in 1850. Their equal width and their X-shape on the chest make them instantly recognisable, but the date of their disappearance means that a mere handful of photographed examples are known.

If a picture shows a soldier in a white waist-belt with two white ammunition pouches and with white braces passing over his shoulders, it's reasonable to conclude that he's wearing the Slade-Wallace equipment, which was introduced in 1888. This became standard infantry-wear for some years, but white leather equipment went out of use in 1908, except in the case of the foot guards, who retained it until the late 1930s.

A flat bag hanging from a cavalry officer's sword-belt was known as a sabretache, and its use was discontinued in 1901. So the presence of a sabretache in a photo gives a latest possible date. But the absence of one provides less clear evidence: the bags were worn with both dress and undress uniform by officers of the light cavalry, with the exception of the hussars, whose officers wore them only as part of their full dress uniform.

The Sam Browne belt has had a long life: it has spread around the world, it continues in use, and a modern reflective version has won the approval of cyclists. But despite its longevity, it can still offer a little help with dating. In its military (rather than road safety) incarnation, it is made of leather and consists of a wide waist belt with a cross-strap passing diagonally over the right shoulder (Figure 16). It was allegedly designed by Lieutenant General Sir Samuel Browne in around 1860. Having lost an arm during the Indian Mutiny, Browne found difficulty in managing his sword, and the cross-strap was used to hold the scabbard steady. The belt came into widespread use by officers in the 1870s and by warrant officers in the 1880s. Until about 1899 it was generally worn with a second cross-strap, but most regiments then switched to a single strap. The few that continued with double straps did so until 1914. So the single cross-strap became common with the dawn of the new century and virtually universal with the outbreak of the Great War. (Technically, according to the Dress Regulations of 1911, there was still justification for two straps, but only when both sword and revolver were being worn.) In the cold and wet conditions often experienced in the trenches, the leather of these belts lost much of its flexibility, so in the years 1914-1918 some officers at the front wore webbing belts instead.

One other feature of some First World War belts was the S-shaped buckle (Figure 12). This was first issued new recruits in 1914, but by 1916 it had become largely obsolete, with its use confined to soldiers in training and certain specialist units.

Rifles

Weapons should properly be classed separately from accoutrements, but since they will receive only brief treatment, they are included in this chapter. Though they figure only rarely in family photographs, they were sometimes taken into the studio, especially in the 19th century. Identification is complicated by the fact that, when a new mechanism was introduced, it was not uncommon for earlier models to be adapted to incorporate it. Nevertheless, a few kinds can be recognised with relative ease. Their latest possible dates are somewhat hazy, but their introduction dates can be relied on.

Introduced in 1853, the muzzle-loading Enfield rifle was adapted in the 1860s to become the Snider (or Snider Enfield) rifle. The Snider was the first breech-loader. Until that date the ammunition had been dropped in at the same point from which it later emerged, but the Snider allowed the round to be loaded at the breech and emerge from the muzzle. Whilst a series of slightly different models was produced, the old Enfield and the new Snider had in common a curved shape on the side of the stock (or wooden part). The area to look at is the just above the trigger, where a long curved shape can be made out (Figure 7). Its ends are rounded, though the rear end may be easier to discern, and the shaping of the wood is often echoed by a metal plate fixed over it. To describe this feature as banana-shaped would not be quite accurate, but to flirt with the comparison would be at least understandable. Above it, about half way along, an almost S-shaped hammer (or striker) stands up. The Snider version was tested and approved in1866 and issued in 1867. It was superseded in 1871, but dwindling numbers remained in the armoury for some years, and a few were still in use in India in the early 1890s.

The Snider's replacement was the Martini-Henry, another single-shot, breech-loading rifle. This had a lever, for ejecting spent rounds, which lay snugly along the underside the stock and behind the trigger guard (Figure 5). This lever was hooked at the end so that it could be easily grasped and operated, and the curve of the hook projected and looked rather like a second trigger guard (but with no trigger cradled within it). The distance between trigger guard and hook varied, since later versions had longer levers, but the illusion of an echoed trigger guard remained. Production of the Martini-Henry began in 1871 and the rifles were widely in service by 1872. From the late 1880s they faced serious competition, but the manufacture of successive models continued, in reduced volumes, into the early 20th century.

Whilst breech-loaders allowed a much faster firing rate than muzzle-loaders, each round still had to be loaded separately. This was changed by the advent of bolt-action rifles, in which the movement of a hand-operated bolt ejected the casing of the old round and allowed the new round to be pushed up into place from a magazine set beneath the breech. The magazine was, in effect, a metal box that clipped into the underside of the rifle just in front of the trigger, and bolt-action rifles can be easily recognised by the fact that part of the magazine was visible, projecting from the underside of the weapon. The first such rifle to enter service in the British army was the Lee-Metford in 1888, and it was the forerunner of a series of Lee-Enfield rifles that were to be used by soldiers in two world wars.

Special cases

Occasionally a uniform is encountered that doesn't seem to fit with the general trend. They are best dealt with separately, and three such cases are considered here.

Camel Corps

The chance of coming across a Camel Corps uniform is not high, since it belonged to a very specific time and place. The body in question is not the Camel Brigade (later the Imperial Camel Corps) that was formed in 1915; it is the force raised in 1884 to travel up the Nile by camel and attempt the rescue of General Gordon in Khartoum. It was drawn from a variety of regiments – with heavy and light cavalry, marines and guards all contributing to its numbers – and two different uniforms appear to have been worn within the corps. Each of these uniforms, if translated by photography into monochrome, is likely to look a little unusual. The less well known of the uniforms was made up of a red serge jumper or tunic, ochre trousers, dark blue puttees and white helmet. The red and white combination on the upper body will appear conventional enough, but the oddly pale trousers and strangely dark puttees will strike a jarring note. The other uniform comprised a grey or greyish blue tunic, pale brown trousers, black boots and a pale brown or khaki helmet and pagri. In monochrome the jacket should look darker than the trousers, but the overall effect will lack both the strongly contrasting shades of pre-khaki clothing and the uniform tone of khaki service dress. The uniforms date from 1884-1885.

Royal Flying Corps

Whilst it was to become a separate service, the air force had its origins within the army. The Balloon Company of the Royal Engineers became part of its Air Battalion in 1911, and this in turn became the Royal Flying Corps in 1912. The RFC uniform featured a double-breasted tunic with a left lapel that pulled across the chest and buttoned into place close to the right shoulder. A side cap completed a distinctive ensemble.

The RFC's growth was initially slow. When, at the end of 1912, questions were asked in the House of Commons about its sluggish advance to war-readiness, the corps had one airship and kite squadron, three aeroplane squadrons and some administrative and training staff. During the First World War, however, personnel rose to a maximum strength of just over 144,000 (which made it much the same size as the Royal Army Medical Corps). In April 1918 the Royal Air Force was formed by combining the RFC with the Royal Naval Air Service, and a new mid-blue uniform with side cap, greyish-blue shirt and black tie was created.

This means that a photograph showing the double-breasted uniform must date from 1912-1918, with the hesitant start making the first two or three years of this period rather less likely.

First World War blues

Photographs from the time of the First World War occasionally show men in clothes of uniform colour that are clearly not the standard khaki issue. Some look like rather ill-fitting lounge suits; some look a little more military, but are too dark-toned to be khaki. In monochrome the darker outfits have much the same tone as blue dress uniforms, but there is nothing very smart, formal or dressy about them. In fact, all of these unconventional uniforms were blue, and they fell into two categories.

The first (and generally paler) category was the 'Hospital Blue' uniform of 1914-1918. This was a set of clothes supplied during their stay to sick or wounded soldiers who found themselves in a military hospital (Figure 14). It was made of blue serge and had pale lapels. It was worn open-necked to show a pale shirt and a red tie (which, in monochrome pictures, tends to look darker than the blue clothing). The lapels are generally the first detail of this uniform to catch the eye.

The second category was the 'Kitchener Blue' uniform, which was worn by some early recruits before the war machine was fully geared up to producing the necessary volume of khaki garments. Kitchener, appointed Minister of War on 4th August 1914, proved a great builder of morale. His recruitment campaign inspired widespread enlistment. So many men were stirred by its slogan – 'Your country needs you' – that it was impossible to equip them all immediately. For some months thousands of new recruits trained in makeshift uniforms and drilled with wooden rifles, and many men had hardly received a real gun and a khaki uniform before they were whisked off to the front. While factories were working overtime to produce the required quantities of khaki cloth, some of the waiting soldiers retained their civilian clothes, and others were kitted out with incomplete or obsolete uniforms. But many of Kitchener's Army were issued temporary uniforms of dark blue serge. Somewhat resembling the hospital uniforms, but without the pale facings and buttoned to the throat, these actually came in two slightly different versions: one was a shade darker and lacked breast pockets. But both belong to the period between September 1914 and September 1915, by which time significant numbers of these newly trained recruits faced their first engagement at the battle of Loos.

Of course, different units received their khaki uniforms at different times. But if a photo of a Great War soldier in khaki is believed to be of a volunteer (rather than a regular), there's a very good chance that the picture dates from well into 1915.

Which end of which war?

Many family historians can count Victorian or Edwardian soldiers among their ancestors, but their numbers are small compared to those with ancestors who fought in one or both world wars. Inevitably, therefore, by far the most common soldier photographs are those relating to these global conflicts. It's natural with such pictures to wish to date them a little more precisely. There is a human interest in wanting to know whether the man in the picture is about face the horrors of war or is reunited with his loved ones. So a little extra focus on photos from these wars seems appropriate.

This chapter brings together, in checklist format, dating clues from 1914-18 and 1939-45. Most clues have already been discussed in detail and are therefore recalled briefly; others are treated to a little more explanation. The topic order of previous chapters is again followed and, in each case, an afterthought about photographic circumstances is appended to the checklist.

If, incidentally, any doubt remains about distinguishing between the two world wars, the basic features of uniform should be remembered. The First World War was a time of tunics, of puttees and of peaked caps for other ranks; the Second World War was a time of blouses, of gaiters and of side caps or berets for other ranks.

First World War

Whole uniform

- 'Kitchener blue' uniforms: September 1914 until about September 1915
- A believed volunteer in khaki: a high chance that 1914 and early 1915 would be too early

Upper body

- Shaggy goatskin (sometimes sleeveless) coat: mainly 1914-1916 (but some soldiers retained them for as long as possible)
- Wool-lined leather jerkin: 1916 or later
- Greatcoat: probably early in the war – say 1914-1915

Lower body
- Boots thickly coated in chalk dust have been ascribed by First World War historian Michael Stedman to the late summer of 1916, when the terrain of the Somme battlefield dried out. So, very dusty boots: probably August or September 1916

Headgear
- Peaked cap with earflaps that could be worn down in cold weather or tied up over the crown when not needed: 1915 or later (less common after 1917)
- Soft, foldable peaked cap with stitched peak: 1917 and later
- Steel helmet: late 1915 or after
- Steel helmet with badge: probably not later than 1917

Hat badges
- Cap with no badge (many early volunteers, having waited a long time for khaki uniforms, eventually received uniforms bearing no insignia): 1914 or 1915
- Unpierced RA badge: 1916-1918

Other arm and shoulder badges
- Geometrical cloth badges: 1915 onwards
- Good conduct/long service stripe (on a war-only soldier): 1916 onwards
- Wound stripe: July 1916 or later
- Overseas service chevron: December 1917 or later

Items worn on the chest
- 1914 Star, or star of indecipherable date: 1917 or later
- 1914-1915 Star: post-war (1919 or later)

Facial hair
- High incidence of heavy moustaches in group photograph: c1900-1914
- Mixed moustaches in group photograph: c1914-1915
- Predominantly clean-shaven group, with some heavy moustaches: middle to late war, c1916-18.

Belts, bags and straps
- S-shaped buckle on belt: generally 1914-1916

In addition to looking for datable details of uniform, it's tempting to speculate on the apparent mood of a picture. Are we looking at a soldier who is apprehensive about the dangers awaiting him at the front, or do we see a soldier who is happy to have survived and to be reunited with his family? The Victorian and Edwardian convention of projecting dignified solemnity still had some currency in studio pictures. But in amateur photos, which were increasing in number, no such inhibitions applied, and smiles were acceptable and even desirable. The problem lies in interpreting the kind of happiness or gravity that is presented to the camera. It's unwise to rely on the easy assumption of nervous seriousness before embarkation and unbridled joy on returning. The soldier who survived the trenches had undergone a terrible experience, and a wan smile of relief may be the best he can muster. The cheerier pictures often show soldiers who don't know what is awaiting them or who, in the course of finding out, are putting a brave face on it. So there are pre-embarkation pictures of men, just kitted out in khaki, who are off to teach the Kaiser a thing or two in a war that is bound to be over by Christmas. They may be striking larky poses with their mates or letting their girlfriend try on their uniform cap. There are pictures, too, of men during off duty moments near the front, who are grinning, smoking, wearing battered caps at rakish angles and holding a placard that says, diplomatically, 'Somewhere in France'. They know by this time what war is like, and their jaunty bravado serves to keep their spirits up. The straight faces and subdued smiles often belong to the soldiers who are home from the front, rather than to those who have yet to go there.

Second World War

The experience of Dunkirk prompted revaluations of various kinds. These included second thoughts about uniform and, particularly, about problems of identifying soldiers in the field. This explains why a significant number of clues date from soon after the withdrawal from France in the late May and early June of 1940.

Upper body
- Old-fashioned khaki tunic on a known Second World War soldier: 1939 or 1940
- 'Jungle green bush' jacket (a tunic rather than a blouse, but made in lightweight fabric for wear in Burma, and provided with four pockets): 1942 onwards

- Signs of economy production measures (such as lack of pocket pleat or pocket flaps) on battledress blouses: 1942 onwards (Figure 18)
- Other ranks pictured off-duty wearing open-necked blouse and visible shirt and tie: September 1944 or later

Headgear
- Wolsley helmet: not later than 1940
- Folding field service cap (side cap): 1939-1943, with some later examples
- Folding side cap in regimental colours rather than khaki (permitted for off-duty wear): 1940 or after, and less frequent after 1943
- Slouch/bush hat (revived in the second half of the war for use in the Far East): c1943 onwards
- Beret: 1943 and after (in most cases)

Hat badges
- Painted regimental markings on steel helmets: after June 1940
- Badge worn very close to the front edge of the side cap (since badges tended to be set further back after the early part of the war): c1939-41

Rank insignia
- Officer's shoulder badge set on a coloured cloth backing: after June 1940

Other arm and shoulder badges
- 'Arm of service' badges (coloured cloth strips) for other ranks, worn high on both sleeves, close to the shoulder: after June 1940
- Divisional badges of cloth (often similar to the simple geometrical arm badges of the First World War): September 1940 and later
- Sleeves noticeably lacking in cloth badges: probably 1939 or first half of 1940
- Cloth arc (identifying regiment) sewn to top of sleeve, close to shoulder seam: 1943 and after
- Overseas service chevrons: February 1944 and later
- Wound stripes: February 1944 and later

Buttons and collar badges

- Brass buttons on a battledress blouse: not later than 1940
- Blouse buttons left uncovered as an economy measure (i.e. not cloth covered, and darker than brass): 1942 onwards (Figure 18)

Belts, bags and straps

- Gas mask carried in case (few were carried by the end of the war): probably pre-1945
- Gas mask case worn hanging by its strap from one shoulder, rather than with strap passed across the chest: probably 1944 (when a lighter model of respirator was introduced)

The Second World War gave rise to a new category of military photo: the soldier as tourist. The First World War soldier may have settled for the security-conscious coyness of pictures identified as 'Somewhere in France', but the Second World War soldier was sometimes snapped by his mates in front of an easily identifiable landmark. This is partly because landmarks punctuated the Second World War soldier's progress through Europe, whereas ground gained by his 1914-18 equivalent was often another frequently contested and (at best) unphotogenic trench. There is, admittedly, an element of simplification to that observation, but topographical photography is more likely occur to a soldier fighting his way across geography than to one fighting his way through geology. So pictures of soldiers in what, to them, were exotic locations date from the time when the Allied Forces were making headway in the later years of the war. It follows that, if a soldier was snapped at a specific site or in a broadly identifiable kind of location, it would be worth finding out when the army was there.

Egyptian and desert photos can be hard to place. The British army was already in Egypt in 1939, part way through a phased withdrawal agreed under an Anglo-Egyptian treaty of 1936. The Italian invasion of Egypt in 1940 simply delayed that withdrawal, so there was in theory a fairly long period of time during which soldiers could be snapped beside the Sphinx or a pyramid. In practice, however, soldier-as-tourist photos were more likely to be taken at the end of a campaign or at relatively comfortable pauses within it. It seems probable that most photos in unspecified desert locations were taken closer to 1943 – when the war in North Africa ended – than to 1940. Recognisably Egyptian pictures could, however, have been taken rather earlier (and even, in some cases, before the beginning of the war).

Identifiable European locations present fewer problems. A soldier cannot have been photographed in a particular location before that location was in Allied hands. It is therefore worth noting that Rome fell in June 1944, that Paris was liberated at the end of August 1944, and that entry into Brussels followed a few days later, in early September.

One final, and perhaps obvious, thought can be applied to soldiers of both wars. Many of them gained promotion during their army service. A high casualty rate could, of course, have the side-effect of a higher promotion rate, but the fact remains that movement up through the ranks takes time. The more stripes a war-only soldier displays, the more time has passed since hostilities began. (In fact, promotion from other ranks to officer was even possible. In the First World War nearly half the newly commissioned officers came up through the ranks, with the incidence of such dramatic rises increasing in the latter years of the conflict.)

The wider picture

Sometimes, especially with pictures from one or other world war, it is possible to date photographs quite precisely from military details. Other soldiers' photos may be harder to pin down, since many items of uniform and equipment were in use for a relatively long time. But, of course, uniform and equipment are not the only possible providers of clues. It can be helpful to recognise the type of photograph and the process used to create it. A cardboard mount can be informative: its thickness, its colour, its design, its corners and its studio information can all give valuable pointers. The studio props and background can suggest a likely date. If a soldier has been photographed with friends or family members, their clothes will have a tale to tell. When clues of these kinds are considered in conjunction with the military details, more exact dating can become possible. It is beyond the scope of this work to discuss all these possibilities, though several books on dating old photographs are listed in the bibliography. For present purposes, the concern is to point out that military details are simply one specialised category of photographic dating clues. The more clues – of any kind – one can find, the more confidently one can estimate a date.

There is, however, one conventional dating tip that may be less applicable to pictures of soldiers. As the second half of the 19th century progressed, studio photographers gradually brought the camera closer to the subject. Full-length shots were characteristic of the 1860s; three-quarter or half-length shots were popular in the 70s and 80s; and head-and-shoulder close-ups dominated the market by the 1890s. This is sometimes also true of soldiers' photographs. But there was a further factor that influenced military portraits: the uniform was a vital part of the subject. There are, therefore, many examples where the photographer has stepped back to take a longer view than is usual for the decade, in order to record a soldier's full martial splendour. The camera has looked at the wider picture just as, in a slightly different sense, the family historian needs to do.

Illustrations

Figure 1: Carte de visite; Bullock Bros, Leamington. Rank-related cuff panels and studio information combine to give a date of c1866-1868. (Carol Craggs collection)

Figure 2: Carte de visite; W Speed, Chester. The side plume and the white belt show that, despite the busby, this is not a hussar. The headdress indicates 1855-1878; the setting suggests the late 1860s. (Carol Craggs collection)

Figure 3: Carte de visite; A Boucher, Brighton. The collar and cuff rank insignia, together with the shako and studio address, give a date of c1876–1878.

Figure 4: Carte de visite; unknown photographer. The hat's regimental number shows this picture was taken before 1881; the facial hair points to a few years earlier. (Carol Craggs collection)

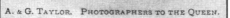

Figure 5: Carte de visite; A & G Taylor, Greenock. The Glengarry cap and Martini-Henry rifle appeared in the 1870s, but shoulder titles came later. Studio dating: c1884. (Carol Craggs collection)

Figure 6: Carte de visite; London & Chester Photo Company, Chester. The Khedive's Star and Egypt Medal point to the 1880s. The cuff trimming may indicate the earlier part of the decade.

Figure 7: Carte de visite; H Clegg, Manchester. The rifle and the blue helmet are consistent with a studio dating of mid-1880s. The Royal Artillery was one regiment that didn't have a star-shaped badge-plate.

Figure 8: Carte de visite; unknown photographer. White overseas helmets appeared in the late 1870s, but the camera's closeness suggests a later date. Sash, metal chinstrap and sharply pointed badge-plate indicate an officer.

Figure 9: Cabinet print; J Adderley, Penicuik, The sergeant wears an NCO's sash over his right shoulder and sports a turn-of-century moustache, His womenfolk's dresses belong to the end of the 1890s.

Figure 10: Postcard; A & G Taylor, London. The hated Broderick caps of these RAMC soldiers were worn between 1902 and 1906.

Figure 11: Postcard; unknown photographer. Between them, the Wolsley helmet, the fixed shoulder strap and the leather leggings point to a date around 1907.

Figure 12: Postcard; H Jenkins, Lowestoft. The S-shaped belt clasp belongs to the First World War's early years, and the pristine cap has not yet seen life at the front.

Figure 13: Postcard; van Ralty, Liverpool, Sheffield, Nottingham, Oldham and Bolton. This soldier's wound stripe cannot date from earlier than July 1916.

Figure 14: Postcard; A Squire, Tooting. The seated soldier wears hospital blues. His companion has a medical orderly's sleeve badge. The back of the photo is dated 'February 15. 1916'.

Figure 15: Postcard; unknown photographer, Trimalgherry, India. The date on the back, '2.7.17', shows that the quilted sola topi was in use years before its formal adoption in 1938.

Figure 16: Postcard; unknown photographer. The de-stiffened hats speak of experience in the trenches, and the date on the back is '26.9.18'. (C. R. Stevenson collection)

Figure 17: Postcard; USA Studios, London. The overseas service stripes show that this picture was not taken earlier than 1918.

Figure 18: Roll film print; unknown photographer. Dated 3ʳᵈ October 1943. The battledress blouse of the centre-front soldier has economy pockets and buttons.

Figure 19: Postcard; unknown photographer. It is 1943 or 1944, but there's no new headgear for this Home Guard anti-aircraft unit, and the officer – like his men – wears a folding side cap.

Figure 20: Roll film print; unknown photographer. The back is marked, 'St Peter's Rome, August 1945'. Some berets are in evidence, as are some side caps in regimental colours.

Bibliography

Military background

I.F.W. Beckett, *Victoria's Wars* (Shire, 1998)

Peter Doyle, *The British Soldier of the First World War* (Shire, 2008)

David Nalson, *The Victorian Soldier* (Shire, 2004)

Mention should also be made of Osprey's *Men-at-Arms* books. The series tends to be most useful in cases where the regiment, the group of regiments or the military campaign is known, but it includes hundreds of titles. Full information can be found at **www.ospreypublishing.com**.

Army uniforms

R.M. Barnes, *A History of the Regiments and Uniforms of the British Army* (Sphere, 1972)

W.Y. Carman, *Richard Simkin's Uniforms of the British Army: The Cavalry Regiments* (Webb & Bower, 1982)

W.Y. Carman, *Richard Simkin's Uniforms of the British Army: The Infantry Regiments* (Webb & Bower, 1985)

Jon Mills, *From Scarlet to Khaki: Understanding the Twentieth Century British Army Uniforms in Your Family Album* (Wardens Publishing, 1998)

Badges, insignia and buttons

Roger W.G. Capewell, *Military Badges for Collectors and Historians* (Roger W.G. Capewell, 2005)

Howard Cole, *Formation Badges of World War I* (Arms & Armour Press, 1973)

Arthur L. Kipling and Hugh L. King, *Head-Dress Badges of the British Army, Volume One: Up to the End of the Great War* (Frederick Muller, 2nd revised edition 1978; republished by The Naval & Military Press, 2006)

W.E. May, W.Y. Carman and John Tanner, *Badges and Insignia of the British Armed Services* (Black, 1974)

Iain Swinnerton, *Identifying your World War I Soldier from Badges and Photographs* (Federation of Family History Societies, 2001, reprinted with amendments 2006)

R.J. Wilkinson-Latham, *Discovering British Military Badges and Buttons* (Shire, 2006)

Researching army ancestors

(This is only a small selection of the titles available)

Simon Fowler, *Tracing Your Army Ancestors* (Pen & Sword, 2006)

Norman Holding, *World War I Army Ancestry* (Federation of Family History Societies, 4th edition updated by Iain Swinnerton, 2004)

William Spencer, *Army Records: A Guide for Family Historians* (The National Archives, 2008)

Iain Swinnerton, *An Introduction to the British Army: its History, Traditions and Records* (Federation of Family History Societies, 1996; reprinted 1998)

Michael J. Watts and Christopher T. Watts, *My Ancestor was in the British Army* (Society of Genealogists, 2009)

General dating of photographs

Audrey Linkman, *The Expert Guide to Dating Victorian Family Photographs* (Greater Manchester County Record Office, 2000)

Robert Pols, *Dating Nineteenth Century Photographs* (Federation of Family History Societies, 2005)

Robert Pols, *Dating Twentieth Century Photographs* (Federation of Family History Societies, 2005)

Jayne Shrimpton, *Family Photographs and How to Date Them* (Countryside Books, 2008)